MW01243352

follow the mekong home

a collection of writings and reflections about
figuring out where home is, identity and culture

krystal m. chuon

Copyright © 2018 by **krystal m. chuon**

All rights reserved. No part of this publication may be reproduced, distributed, or transmitted in any form or by any means, including photocopying, recording, or other electronic or mechanical methods, without the prior written permission of the publisher, except in the case of brief quotations embodied in critical reviews and certain other noncommercial uses permitted by copyright law. For permission requests, please email:

krystalchuon@gmail.com

Cover Layout: Adaeze (Noah) Durunna

follow the mekong home/ krystal m. chuon. -- 1st ed.
ISBN-13: 978-1726313797
ISBN-10: 1726313794

dedicated to my khmer/krom community,
especially those who are still trying to figure out
what it means to be khmer

how does it feel
to have grown
from the soil
beneath your feet
only to be told that
the land you have ever known
no longer
        belongs
                to you?

krystal m. chuon

this land is *ramaytush ohlone*
san francisco

my land is *kampuchea/krom*
cambodia/vietnam

years of learning about the indigenous of
america

that i never stopped to question my own
indigenous identity

ma, *yeay* and *tha*
khmer krom

inhabited the mekong delta long before
the vietnamese came down
ancestral lands steeped in history and
importance

the start of a civilization
that has been forgotten
by the
majority

i realized that
you can't fully learn
about cambodia
until you learn
about *kampuchea krom*

that's where it all started
that's where the story of
our lineage

begins

i knew about
the khmer rouge
tuol sleng
choeung ek

but nobody told me about
the vinh te canal
dug up by the labor of the khmer krom
who were overworked

and how all the laborers died
by purposeful flooding

which led to the story of
not spilling the master's tea
or remembered as
brayat kampub te ong

innocent bodies
buried up to their necks
their heads used
to balance
as a stove
to boil the vietnamese's tea

the pain
the cries
the struggle as death neared

and the last thing they hear is

be careful not to spill the master's tea!

krystal m. chuon

growing up and learning about who i was
i always managed to find a group
who would discredit
the contributions
inventions
and artistry
of the khmers

i went through it again
as i read more on khmer krom history
seeing how people said
kampuchea krom was just all jungle
and the indigenous khmer krom
were actually refugees in their own land!

even with evidence,
tangible evidence,
we're made to feel nonexistent
stripped of our heritage
by people who wants to alter history
to fit their delusional narratives

i, and my people, are too proud
of our indigenous bloodline

to be affected
by their nonsense

it's time they listen to what
we
have to say!

"i have pride to be born as khmer"

follow the mekong home

i will never be whole

    until i caress the earth

that birthed my people

june 4, 1949
france cedes kampuchea krom
to vietnam
they claim our land was always theirs
but the indigenous doesn't lie

we know whose land it is
we know how the river flows
and when it floods
we know why we farm here
and not there

or why we build our homes like this
and not like those colonizers
and why we give names like prey nokor
"forest city"
to our ancestral lands...

we *know* our land
we *love* our land
we *bleed* for our land
and it's freedom
that we seek
for *our* land

follow the mekong home

ancestry dot com

23 and me
and you
and her
and him
and them

and that one *oum* who lives by the river

i don't need some website

    to categorize me

      to analyze me

    to figure out my ancestry

i know where

i come from

i wonder who these women are
adorned in elaborate jewelry
their eyes open
seeing
observing
cameras capturing their beauty

over a thousand devatas
covering the walls
of angkor wat
as well as other temples across the country
and beyond
and yet,
no one has a clue

some may be queens
servants
or every day women
artists
dancers
mothers
a relative

with their ornate crowns

and flowers tucked in just right

from a golden era, long, long gone
these women stay
frozen in position
stuck in
an eternal mystery

4, 500 ways of showing fear
sadness
triumph
pain
happiness

hands bent back
fingers in position
sometimes representing a leaf
a flower
or a fruit

chest forward
one leg up, a balancing act
as the dancer turns
with a slight smile
to face a crowd in awe

it is truly a blessing
to witness an art
that arose centuries ago
and was threatened of being erased
from our memories

and yet, here it is

with its 4, 500 gestures
representing the complexity of human
emotion

an ancient art form
that continues to tell the tales

of long ago

follow the mekong home

having traveled to cambodia 4 times
and often staying for an entire month
solidified it as second home to me

on the night that trump won,
i no longer felt safe
american soil now felt like a cage
that i wanted so desperately to escape

i no longer felt any attachment
to this country
to the only state i've lived in since birth
i felt, at this point, anywhere but here
would make a better home

i want to glide my fingers along the tonlé sap

ride in the tuk tuk while the sun dips into
the horizon

as it casts a warm glow

on children playing in front of the royal
palace

i want to be at the top of the mountains

out of breath, lungs about to burst

gasping for air as i stare in amazement

at the beautiful country beneath me

other mountains, temples, and wooden
homes

as far as the eye can see

landscapes so etched into my memory

but in fleeting moments

i ponder

if i was ever there

at all

the mekong river
trickles through cambodia
bypassing an imaginary border
until its arm reaches
kampuchea krom

diverging into the ocean
with its spindly fingers as if
firmly holding on
to the land
set astray

just one important piece
to cambodia's
puzzle

about the writer

krystal m. chuon grew up writing and illustrating fictional stories. she later turned to creating zines, sharing about her life through poetry, prose and collages.

when she's not writing, you can find her creating art, reading books and watching too many different TV shows all at once.

krystal currently resides in california.

———

find her:

monyda.com

Made in the USA
Middletown, DE
07 October 2022

11940388R00019